Contents

Words that appear in **bold** can be found in the glossary on page 46.

The Threat of War

In 1933, Adolf Hitler became the leader of Germany. He promised to make the country powerful again. After the First World War ended in 1918, Germany had had some of its lands taken away and given to other countries. Hitler was determined to get those lands back. He began to build up his army and air force.

Britain and France did not do anything to stop Hitler at first. He took over the Rhineland and made Austria part of Germany. He marched into part of Czechoslovakia and a

Above German soldiers march past Adolf Hitler (centre, in front of chair) at a parade, in 1939.

few months later seized the whole country. By now, the governments of Britain and France were very worried. They said that if Hitler attacked Poland, they would declare war on Germany.

On 1 September 1939 Germany invaded Poland. Britain and France warned Hitler to remove his troops by 11 a.m. on 3 September. The deadline passed. Hitler had ignored it.

The War Years
The Home Front

Alison Cooper

WAYLAND

Titles in this series:
The Home Front
Wartime Cookbook

Picture acknowledgements:
AKG London 12 top, 20, 21 top; Camera Press 4, 39 top, 45 top; Corbis cover background; Imperial War Museum cover main; title page, 5 top; 6 bottom, 7 top, 8, 9 both, 10, 11 all, 13, 14 all, 17 both, 19 bottom, 21 bottom, 22, 23 top, 24, 25 both, 27 top, 28, 29 both, 35 bottom, 36 bottom, 38, 40, 41 bottom, 42 bottom, 43, 44; Magnum Photos Inc 34, 37; Peter Newark's Historical Pictures 12 bottom, 15 top, 18, 19 top, 39 bottom; Popperfoto 27 bottom; Range / Bettmann / UPI 35 top; Mr Carel Toms 30, 32, 33 both; The Wayland Picture Library contents page, 15 bottom. The artwork on page 30 was supplied by Malcolm Walker.

Cover: A boy is more interested in his toy car than the unexploded bomb down the street.
Title page: Young evacuees about to leave the city.
Contents page: Bomb damage in central London.

This book is based on the original title *The War Years: The Home Front* by Brian Moses. First published in Great Britain in 1995 by Wayland (Publishers) Ltd

This differentiated text version by Alison Cooper, published in 2005 by Hodder Wayland, an imprint of Hodder Children's Books

This paperback edition published in 2007 by Wayland, an imprint of Hachette Children's Books

© Wayland 2005

Wayland, an imprint of Hachette Children's Books, 338 Euston Road, London NW1 3BH

Original designer: Malcolm Walker
Layout for this edition: Simon Borrough
Editor for this edition: Hayley Leach

British Library Cataloguing in Publication Data
Cooper, Alison, 1967-
        The home front. – (The war years)
        1.World War, 1939-1945 – Great Britain – Juvenile
        literature 2.Great Britain – History – George VI, 1936-1952
        -Juvenile literature 3.Great Britain –Social conditions –
        20th century – Juvenile literature
        I.Title
        941'.084

ISBN-10: 0 7502 5119 0
ISBN-13: 978 0 7502 5119 8

Printed in China

The British Prime Minister, Neville Chamberlain, made a radio announcement to the British people. He told them Britain was at war.

*'Almost immediately afterwards we were horrified to hear for the first time the dismal wailing of an **air-raid siren**. It was a false alarm but initially terrifying.'*
The Day War Broke Out
by Peter Haining

The Second World War had begun. It was to last until 1945. All of the world's most powerful countries, and many less powerful ones, became involved.

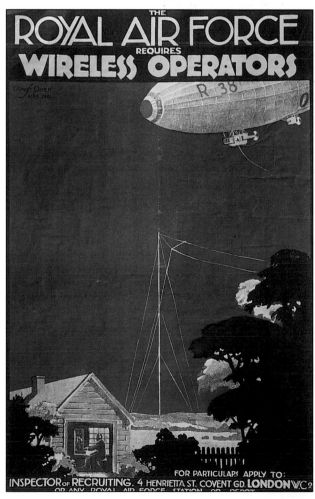

Preparations for War

Left Gas masks covered the whole face, with a clear section so that people could see where they were going.

Below Children under the age of two were given containers that covered their entire bodies to protect them from gas attacks.

The British government expected German aeroplanes to bomb towns and cities if war broke out. They thought the Germans might even drop bombs containing poison gas.

When it seemed likely that there was going to be a war, they began to give out gas masks to everyone in Britain. People had to carry their gas masks with them all the time and practise putting them on quickly. The masks were uncomfortable to wear for more than a few minutes.

The government also gave out Anderson shelters, where people could hide during a bombing raid. These were made of curved corrugated iron sheets. People set them up in their gardens and then piled earth over the top to give more protection from bomb blasts.

People who did not have a garden tried to make a safe area inside their home, such as a cupboard under the stairs or a basement.

Above These children are climbing into their Anderson shelter.

When the war began, many people volunteered to help if there were air raids. Some people trained as **air-raid wardens**. It was their job to help people get to a shelter during an attack. Once the attack was over, they helped to organize rescue services.

Left This poster asks men to become air-raid wardens, but this important job was also done by women.

Moving to Safety

Everyone was worried about what would happen when the Germans began to bomb Britain's cities. Months before the war began, the government started planning to **evacuate** children. The children would leave their homes and move to safer places in the countryside.

The government called its plan Operation Pied Piper. Children under five were to be evacuated with their mothers. Older children were to travel with their teachers. People living in country areas would be paid to look after the **evacuees**.

Above These young children are being evacuated with their mothers.

Evacuation began on the day the Germans invaded Poland. Over the next few days, more than one million women and children left British cities. There were many tears as children and their parents were separated. No one knew if they would ever see one another again.

Left Many children, like these boys, were evacuated by train.

Below Mothers crowded round the station barriers for a last look at their children.

At the end of their long journey, the evacuees waited to find out who would offer a home to them.

The villagers … came to choose which children they wanted. I noticed boys of about twelve went very quickly – perhaps to help on the farm. Eventually only my friend Nancy and myself were left … A large, happy-looking, middle-aged lady rushed in asking, 'Is that all you have left? … I'll take the poor bairns.'

No Time to Say Goodbye
by Ben Wicks

9

Country Life

Families who gave homes to poor city children were often shocked by the new arrivals. Many of the **evacuees** had head lice or skin diseases such as scabies. Some were not used to eating meals at a table. This evacuee explains how different his new surroundings were from his home in London:

Everything was so clean in the room. We were even given flannels and toothbrushes. We'd never cleaned our teeth up till then. And hot water came from the tap.

The World is a Wedding *by Bernard Kops*

Left This elderly woman took in six young evacuees.

Right There was not enough room in local schools for all the evacuee children. This group are having a lesson outside.

Some evacuees went to live with families who were poorer than their own families. They had to get used to living in farm cottages with no electricity and an outdoor toilet.

Below These evacuees are arriving in New York, USA.

Many of the children who were **evacuated** had never been on a holiday, or travelled far from their city homes. They loved exploring the countryside and helping out on the farms. But some were homesick and very unhappy.

A small number of children were evacuated to other countries, such as Australia. But a ship carrying evacuees was sunk by a **U-boat** in 1940. After that, parents stopped sending their children abroad.

The Blackout

From 1 September 1939, Britain's villages, towns and cities were in complete darkness every night. No one was allowed to show any lights, in case it helped enemy aircraft to work out where to drop bombs. This was called the blackout. People covered the windows of their homes with heavy curtains, or thick paper so that no light shone into the streets. Street lamps were not used.

Above These people are putting up their blackout curtains.

Left This poster warns people to take extra care if they have to go outside at night.

Left In the blackout it was almost impossible for drivers to spot farm animals on the road. This woman is painting white stripes on a cow to make it easier to see.

Months passed and no bombs fell. More people were injured in road accidents in the dark streets than by enemy bombing. They tried all sorts of ways to keep themselves safe:

White lines were painted along kerbs and men were encouraged to leave their white shirt tails hanging out at night. A local farmer painted white stripes on his cows in case they strayed on to the roads.

War Boy: A Country Childhood
by Michael Foreman

In the summer of 1940, bombing raids began. **Air-raid wardens** walked around the streets, making sure that no lights were showing. People could be fined for letting their lights show.

Rationing

Britain depended on goods that were brought to the country by ship. These included food, fuel and materials for use in factories. As soon as the war started, **U-boats** began to sink ships carrying goods to Britain.

The British government introduced **rationing** to make sure that everyone could have a fair share of the food that was available. Everybody was given a ration book and allowed to buy a certain amount of food each week.

People tried to grow as much food for themselves as they could. Any spare bit of land was used to grow vegetables, or to keep some chickens or a pig. Farmers worked long hours to grow and harvest more crops.

Above A shopkeeper marks a ration book to show that the customer has bought her weekly ration.

Below Even London's parks were used to grow food.

From June 1940, new clothes were rationed. Precious space on the ships could not be used to carry clothing fabric, and workers were needed for essential war jobs, not for making clothes. People had to make their clothes last as long as possible. Children often wore clothes made from adults' old clothes.

This poster reminds people not to waste fuel.

Wartime Food Rations for an Adult

Bacon and ham: 4 oz (100 g) per week
Meat: to the value of 1 shilling 2 pence (6p today) per week
Butter: 2 oz (50 g) per week
Cheese: 2 oz (50 g), sometimes it rose to 4 oz (100 g) per week
Margarine: 4 oz (100 g) per week
Cooking fat: 4 oz (100 g) often dropping to 2 oz (50 g) per week
Milk: 3 pints (1.8 litres), often dropping to 2 pints (1.2 litres) per week
Dried milk: one packet every 4 weeks
Sugar: 8 oz (225 g) per week
Jam: 1 lb (450 g) every 2 months
Tea: 2 oz (50 g) per week
Eggs: 1 egg per week, sometimes dropping to 1 egg every 2 weeks
Dried eggs: one packet every 4 weeks
Sweets: 12 oz (350 g) every 4 weeks

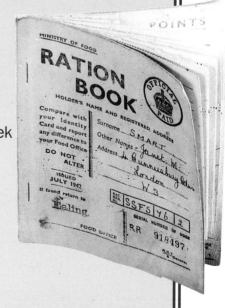

We'll Eat Again: A Collection of Recipes from the War Years by Marguerite Patten

'Doing their bit'

In the summer of 1940, it seemed very likely that the Germans would try to invade Britain. They had conquered France and were building up their army on the French coast, just a few kilometres across the English Channel. The British government set up the Local Defence Volunteers, or Home Guard, to help the **armed forces** if there was an invasion.

The Home Guard was made up mainly of men who were too old or too young to join the armed forces. They were all volunteers, who trained to fight when they were not doing their everyday jobs. At first, they had no uniforms or proper weapons. They trained with old shotguns, garden forks and knives fixed to broom handles.

Above These members of the Home Guard have weapons but no uniforms.

Left These boys are filling sacks with rubbish. The rubbish was sorted, and useful items were taken out so that they could be reused or recycled.

Everyone was encouraged to 'do their bit' to help Britain win the war. One way of helping was to collect scrap metal. People collected tonnes of old saucepans, tin cans and even iron railings from parks and gardens.

Your railing will be melted down to make ships, shells, guns, tanks and aircraft, and thus will help win this war.

Ministry of Supply leaflet

Below This mountain of saucepans was collected so that they could be melted down to make aircraft.

In fact, most of the metal that was collected was not suitable for making tanks and aircraft, so it was never used. But people did not know this at the time. They were proud of the efforts they had made.

The Battle of Britain

Germany defeated France in May 1940 and prepared to attack Britain. The Germans' first task was to defeat the Royal Air Force (RAF). Once they had done this, their invasion ships could cross the English Channel without being attacked from the air.

Below This Italian poster shows Italian and German planes attacking targets in Britain.

The Battle of Britain began in August 1940. Day after day, German bombers attacked ports and airfields in southern England. RAF pilots in **Hurricanes** and **Spitfires** tried to shoot down the enemy before they could reach their targets.

Games at school were . . . enlivened by dog-fights between aircraft overhead and it was sometimes necessary to run for cover as a stream of bullets ploughed across the pitch.

Children of the Blitz
by Robert Westall

Left These fighter pilots are having a rest before they have to take to the air again.

Below This poster includes the most famous words from Churchill's speech. 'The many' are the British people, who owe their survival to the fighter pilots – 'the few'.

After several weeks of German attacks, many RAF planes had been shot down. The pilots who were left were exhausted. Then, just when it seemed the RAF could not fight on any longer, the attacks on their airfields stopped. Hitler had decided to attack large cities instead.

Winston Churchill, the British Prime Minister, made a speech in Parliament. He praised the RAF pilots for saving Britain from invasion.

"NEVER WAS SO MUCH OWED BY SO MANY TO SO FEW" *THE PRIME MINISTER*

The Blitz on London

In the autumn of 1940, bombing raids on London began. These raids were known as the Blitz. The bombers came at night because darkness made it harder for British aircraft and guns on the ground to shoot them down.

The Germans wanted to destroy London's factories and fuel supplies. They also hoped that the raids would make people so tired and miserable that they would want to **surrender**. People did become very tired – but they were also determined not to give up.

Below These houses have been destroyed in a bombing raid and a bus has toppled into a bomb crater in the road.

In every heart there is not fear, only a . . . hatred of the enemy and a determination to carry on at all costs.
  Winston Churchill, from the *Daily Herald* newspaper, 16 November 1940

The Blitz lasted from September 1940 to May 1941. Thousands of people lost their homes. Firefighters struggled to control huge blazes and rescue workers searched damaged buildings for people who were trapped. **Searchlights** swept the sky, trying to catch enemy bombers in their powerful beam. Then **anti-aircraft guns** began to fire into the night sky.

Above Some areas of London were completely flattened.

Left Barrage balloons prevented enemy bombers from flying low over their targets. These barrage balloons are flying above Buckingham Palace.

The Blitz across Britain

Soon after the raids on London began, the Germans began to bomb other cities. They chose important ports, such as Southampton and Liverpool. They wanted to destroy ships in harbour, the yards where ships were built and the warehouses where vital supplies were stored.

Below Coventry Cathedral was destroyed in the raid of 14 November 1940.

Industrial areas, like the West Midlands, were hard hit too. On the night of 14 November 1940, the enemy's target was Coventry. By the following morning, much of the town was in ruins. King George VI visited the area and wrote in his diary:

Poor Coventry! I was horrified at the sight of the centre of the town...
The water, electricity, and gas services had stopped working ...
The people in the street wondered where they were ... nothing could
be recognized.

Left People trudge through a Glasgow street, with damaged houses all around them.

Some of Britain's most important shipyards were along the River Clyde around Glasgow. They too were heavily bombed. There were 12,000 houses in Clydebank before the attacks began. Only eight were left undamaged. More than 50,000 people were made homeless.

Below A woman factory worker is rescued from a bombed building.

People worked hard to repair the damage and often showed great courage:

*My sister and I . . . ran up into the house and there was an **incendiary bomb** blazing like mad in the middle of the couch. And she got the coal shovel and I got a basin and we lifted it into the basin and chucked it out the window. So that saved the house going on fire . . .*

The Greenock Blitz
(*Inverclyde District Libraries, 1991*)

Life in the Shelters

When enemy bombers were on their way, **air-raid sirens** began to wail across towns and cities. Some families hurried out to the Anderson shelter in their garden (see pages 6–7). Raids often lasted for several hours, so people tried to make their shelters as comfortable as they could. Many people did not have a garden. They scrambled under the Morrison shelter – which was like a big metal table – in their kitchen and huddled together.

Some people did not have any shelter of their own:

My father wouldn't have an air-raid shelter. He said it would take up too much room in his garden . . . When the Blitz started we were all under the dining-room table complete with dog.

The Greenock Blitz (*Inverclyde District Libraries, 1991*)

Right These people are going to shelter in tunnels cut out of the cliffs at Ramsgate.

People who did not have their own shelter could use the public shelters, or more unusual places. Hundreds of Londoners took the train each evening to the Chislehurst Caves outside the city, where they could sleep in safety. In Northfleet, east of London, people sheltered in tunnels that had been dug to link chalk quarries.

Thousands of people spent the night on the platforms of London Underground stations. When the electric current that ran through the rails was turned off, some people even slept on the tracks.

'Keep Smiling Through'

People had so many worries during the war. There was the constant fear that family members or friends might be killed, the dangers of the Blitz and the everyday struggle to make the rations last out. A visit to the cinema or a night at a dance hall gave them the chance to forget their worries for a little while.

Below The singer Vera Lynn became known as the 'Forces Sweetheart'.

The most popular film during the war was *Gone with the Wind*. This is a love story as well as a tale about the American Civil War. Children enjoyed adventure films such as *Tarzan, Flash Gordon* and *The Lone Ranger*.

Many wartime songs had words that gave people hope and courage. One of the most popular ones was 'We'll Meet Again', which encouraged people to 'keep smiling through'.

Television broadcasts had begun in the 1930s but the television service was closed down during the war. People listened to the radio or watched newsreels at the cinema to find out how the war was going.

The singer Vera Lynn presented a radio show called *Sincerely Yours*. People could write to her with messages and song requests for men and women in the **armed forces**. For children, there was a programme called *Children's Hour*, presented by Uncle Mac. He always ended his programme with the words 'Goodnight children everywhere'.

Women at War

Many men left their everyday jobs to join the **armed forces**, and women took over their work. Often, these were jobs that women had never done before, such as building ships and assembling aircraft. The Women's Land Army provided workers to help on farms. They ploughed fields, milked cows, cut hedges and brought in the harvest.

Women spent long hours doing hard, heavy work but they were never paid as much as the men. For many women, though, war work gave them opportunities they had never had before.

For the first time I had some . . . freedom from my parents' control; I had money of my own . . . and I was being given responsibilities and treated like an adult.

Dorothy Harris, personal memories

WOMEN OF BRITAIN
COME INTO THE FACTORIES
ASK AT ANY EMPLOYMENT EXCHANGE FOR ADVICE AND FULL DETAILS

Above This poster encourages women to help the war effort by going to work in a factory.

Women who joined the armed forces were not allowed to take part in fighting. They did other essential jobs, such as flying new aircraft from factories to airfields, decoding enemy radio signals and aiming **anti-aircraft guns**. They drove heavy lorries and repaired vehicles that broke down. They also did traditional 'women's work', such as cooking and clerical work.

Above These women are working in a shipyard.

Many women who were not doing paid war work joined the Women's Voluntary Service (WVS). The WVS provided food and blankets for people bombed out of their homes. They ran canteens and helped with evacuation.

Right These women belong to the Auxiliary Territorial Service, which was the women's branch of the army. They are learning how to show the position of enemy bombers.

German Invasion: The Channel Islands

The Channel Islands are a group of small islands in the English Channel. Although they are near the coast of France, they actually belong to Britain.

In 1940, Hitler was keen to take control of the Channel Islands. He was worried that Britain might use the islands to launch attacks on his armies in France. He also wanted to show the British government that he could conquer British territory. His next target would be Britain itself.

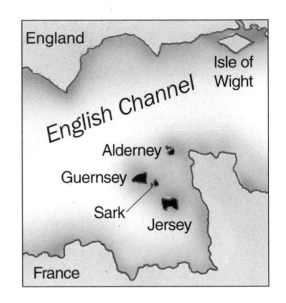

Left The Channel Islands were an easy target for Hitler's army.

Left German soldiers parade through St Peter Port on Guernsey.

The German attack began with a bombing raid on 28 June 1940. Molly Bihet, who was eight years old at the time, lived in St Peter Port on Guernsey. She saw the planes coming in low over the harbour.

We gave them a wave with a cucumber we'd just bought ... but soon ran for shelter as they were German planes which started to machine gun and bomb the ships and the harbour.

A Child's War *by Molly Bihet*

Two days later, German soldiers landed on Jersey and Guernsey, the largest islands. The soldiers were happy and excited. They were sure that their army would soon invade Britain.

Above To celebrate their victory, these soldiers are taking the flag of Guernsey back to Germany.

Below The German flag flies over a building on Jersey.

German Rule

The people of the Channel Islands had to get used to life under German rule. Some tried, in secret, to make life difficult for the enemy. Painting 'V' signs on walls was one way of showing their defiance. The 'V' stood for Victory, meaning victory for Britain in the war.

The Germans took away the islanders' radios, to prevent them listening to British news about the war. Some people managed to hide their radios and listened in secret to the BBC. One Jersey man and his son were caught. They were sent to a German prison camp, where they both died.

Food, fuel and clothing were in short supply. The islanders were forced to invent strange recipes using whatever food they could get. For example, they used barley carrots and parsnips to make a drink that they called 'coffee'. Children sometimes managed to get food from the Germans.

Above The Germans put up notices like these to try to stop people painting 'V' signs around the islands.

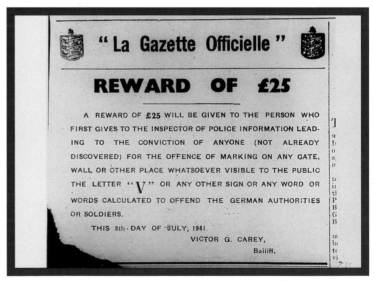

"La Gazette Officielle"

REWARD OF £25

A REWARD OF £25 WILL BE GIVEN TO THE PERSON WHO FIRST GIVES TO THE INSPECTOR OF POLICE INFORMATION LEADING TO THE CONVICTION OF ANYONE (NOT ALREADY DISCOVERED) FOR THE OFFENCE OF MARKING ON ANY GATE, WALL OR OTHER PLACE WHATSOEVER VISIBLE TO THE PUBLIC THE LETTER "V" OR ANY OTHER SIGN OR ANY WORD OR WORDS CALCULATED TO OFFEND THE GERMAN AUTHORITIES OR SOLDIERS.

THIS 8th-DAY OF JULY, 1941

VICTOR G. CAREY,

Bailiff.

Left This cinema on Guernsey is showing a German film. There is a picture of Adolf Hitler above the door.

We would pick up potatoes (mostly rotten) from the street while the Germans were unloading stores.
Liberation *by Nick Machon*

The situation got worse as the war went on. Some reports said that islanders were forced to eat cats and dogs to avoid starvation.

Left Harbours were surrounded with barbed wire, in case islanders tried to escape by boat.

Americans in Britain

In December 1941, Japan launched a surprise attack on the USA. Shortly afterwards, Germany, which was allied to Japan, declared war on the USA. American forces were soon on their way to join Britain in the fight against Germany.

Late in 1942 the traffic past our shop began to include trucks and jeeps of the USAF [United States Air Force]. We used to run behind the trucks . . . and shout, 'Got any gum, chum?'
War Boy: A Country Childhood *by Michael Foreman*

Below An American soldier plays with British children whose parents had been killed in the war.

The American soldiers often gave out supplies of sweets and chocolate that they were sent from home. Children loved the new arrivals. Many British women fell in love with them, too. Some women married their American boyfriends and after the war they made new homes in the USA.

By the spring of 1944, there were more than a million American troops in Britain. Southern England was like a huge army camp. Roads were jammed with military vehicles. The **Allies** were preparing to cross the English Channel and attack the German forces in France. The invasion began on 6 June 1944. This was D-Day.

Above These American soldiers are donating their sweets to British children for Christmas.

Left American soldiers in a military hospital join a group of entertainers in a song around the piano.

Wartime Childhood

Many of the children who were **evacuated** at the start of the war returned home after a few months. Parents and children were unhappy because they were separated and there was no bombing at first. When the Blitz did begin, children shared the terrifying experience.

One boy remembered going to school and finding out that friends had been killed in the air raids:

Above The boys in this school have their gas masks on the desks, in case of a gas attack.

The names would go up on the blackboard – all your friends that had been killed. We used to say a little prayer and hope it would be different the next night, but it wasn't.

A People's War *by Peter Lewis*

Left This boy is more interested in fixing his toy car than in the unexploded bomb further down the street.

At many schools, the air-raid shelters were not big enough to hold all the children at one time. Some children went to school only in the mornings and the others went in the afternoons, to make sure there would be room for everyone in the shelter if there was an air raid. Children did not learn as quickly as children had learnt before the war.

Left This young boy in the East End of London is wearing a tin hat for protection.

Doodlebugs and Rockets

The Allied invasion of France (see page 35) was a success. People in Britain began to hope that the war would soon be over. It was a tremendous shock when bombs began to fall once more.

Britain had not suffered severe bombing since 1942. It had become too difficult for the German bombers to reach their targets. But, secretly, the Germans had developed a new weapon. It was the V1 aeroplane, which became known as the flying bomb or 'doodlebug'.

Doodlebugs did not have pilots. They were launched towards Britain from sites in France. When they ran out of fuel, they plunged to the ground and the explosives they were carrying blew up.

LEAVE THIS TO US SONNY — YOU OUGHT TO BE OUT OF LONDON

MINISTRY OF HEALTH EVACUATION SCHEME

Above Doodlebugs hit London, Kent and Sussex most often. Once again, the government encouraged parents to send their children to safer areas.

People knew when a doodlebug was about to drop because the sound of its engine stopped. It gave them a little time to try to take cover. But in September 1944, a more deadly weapon began to strike London. The V2 was a type of rocket. It flew too fast for planes or **anti-aircraft guns** to shoot it down. The only way to stop the V2s was to destroy their launch sites.

Above Homes in London destroyed by a doodlebug.

Below A V2 rocket at its launch site in France.

The End of the War

The V1s and the V2s (see pages 38–9) hit Britain hard but across Europe the Germans were steadily being pushed back. **Soviet** troops were attacking them in the east, while British and American forces attacked from the west.

Left Soldiers seized the newspapers announcing the victory over Germany as soon as they rolled off the printing press.

American and Soviet soldiers met up near Berlin, the German capital, on 25 April 1945. The Germans **surrendered** a few days later. On 8 May, the **Allies** celebrated Victory in Europe (VE) day.

All over Britain, people held parties in the streets. In London, crowds surrounded Buckingham Palace, cheering the King and Queen and Winston Churchill. Everyone was full of joy and relief that the war was over.

In the Channel Islands, 9 May 1945 was Liberation Day. The German soldiers on the islands surrendered and British troops landed. One woman remembered the day like this:

I think Liberation was the happiest day of our lives… I saw the English troops marching along the Front with all their kit. It was a very hot summer day. There were kisses for them, chocolate for us and such a feeling of thankfulness.

Liberation *by Nick Machon*

Above Thousands of people gathered in Trafalgar Square in London to celebrate VE Day.

Below Liberation Day in the Channel Islands.

Returning Home

Left Metal prefabs like this one in Surrey could be built quickly and cheaply to provide homes.

Below Villagers say goodbye to evacuees who are going back to London.

The end of the war brought families together again. **Evacuees** returned from the country. Nearly two million soldiers, sailors and airmen came home. Many barely recognized the children who ran to welcome them, after so many years apart.

Not everyone had a home to which they could return. So many houses had been damaged or destroyed by bombs. Thousands of prefabricated houses, or 'prefabs', were built to try to solve the problem.

Often, people did not find family life easy after the war. Family members and friends had been killed or injured. Many women had lost their husbands and struggled to bring up their children alone.

Above These teenagers spent the war in Australia and have just arrived back in Britain.

Some evacuees had enjoyed life in the country more than life in the cities. Others had grown to love their **foster parents** and missed them very much. Evacuees whose parents had been killed in the war were sometimes adopted by their foster parents.

Although there were problems, there was also great hope for the future. Vera Lynn, the 'Forces Sweetheart' (see page 26), described her feelings like this:

I thought of those who had been dear to us who had not lived to see this . . . and then went indoors to stand looking at the sleeping faces of my two little sons, whose lives lay before them in a world of peace.

We'll Meet Again *by Vera Lynn with Robin Cross and Jenny de Gex*

After the War

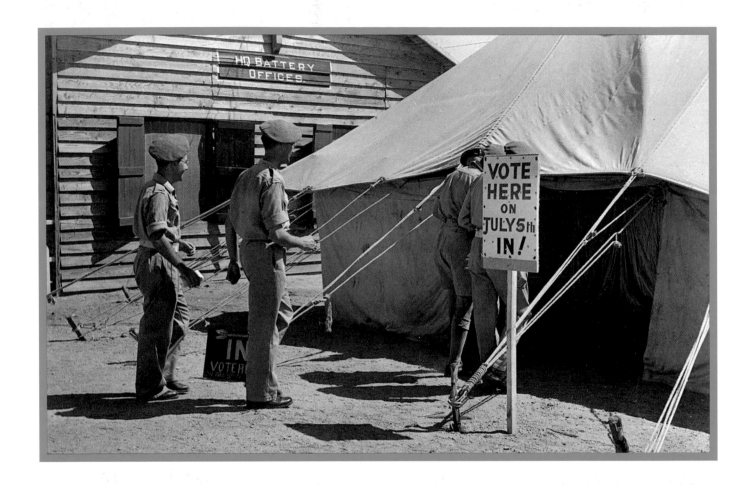

Winston Churchill had been a great leader. But two months after the war in Europe ended, he was no longer Prime Minister. His party, the Conservatives, were defeated in the **general election** of July 1945. The Labour Party won because people believed they would do a better job of rebuilding Britain.

Britain was very poor after the war. It took years to rebuild damaged cities. **Rationing** had to continue. Some foods, such as bread, had to be rationed for the first time.

Above People who were serving overseas in the **armed forces** were still able to vote in the 1945 election. These soldiers are voting near Cairo, in Egypt.

Although the war in Europe was over, British and American forces were still fighting Japan. In August 1945, the USA dropped **atomic bombs** on the cities of Hiroshima and Nagasaki. Japan **surrendered** a few days later. One man wrote in his diary:

…the hell of war, the killing, the misery is over.

We'll Meet Again *by Vera Lynn, with Robin Cross and Jenny de Gex*

Above Clement Attlee (second from left) took over from Winston Churchill (centre) at the 1945 election.

Below Four years after the war ended, people still had to queue for their meat rations.

Glossary

Air-raid siren A warning siren that was sounded when enemy aircraft were on the way. The air-raid warning was a wailing noise that rose and fell.

Air-raid warden A person who made sure people did not show lights after dark, helped people to get to air-raid shelters and helped to organize emergency services after a raid.

Allies Britain, the USA and the Soviet Union, which were the main countries that fought together against Germany, Italy and Japan.

Anti-aircraft guns Large guns that were positioned around likely targets, such as cities. The gunners tried to shoot down enemy aircraft.

Armed forces The navy, army and air force.

Atomic bombs Bombs that get their incredible explosive power from the splitting of atoms (the basic 'building blocks' that make up everything that exists). They have never been used in war, except at the end of the Second World War.

Dog-fights Fights between two or more aircraft, with the aircraft flying close to one another and trying to shoot each other down.

Evacuate To move to a place of safety.

Evacuees People who are moved to a place of safety.

Foster parents People who take children into their own homes to look after them.

General election An election held across the whole country. People vote for their Member of Parliament (MP) and the party that gets most MPs can form the government.

Hurricane A type of British fighter aircraft, flown by a single pilot.

Incendiary bomb A bomb that is designed to start fires when it lands.

Rationing Making sure that everyone gets an equal share of the goods available.

Searchlights Powerful lights that were used to search the night sky for enemy aircraft. Once an aircraft had been lit up by the searchlight, anti-aircraft gunners would try to shoot it down.

Soviet Belonging to the Soviet Union, a country that was made up of modern Russia and several other countries in northern Europe and central Asia.

Spitfire A type of British fighter aircraft, flown by a single pilot.

Surrender To give up fighting.

U-boat A German submarine.

Ukelele A small stringed instrument.

Further Information

Books to Read

At Home in World War Two: The Blitz by Stewart Ross (Evans Books Ltd, 2004)

Britain in World War II: Rationing by Alison Cooper (Hodder Wayland, 2004)

History Through Newspapers: The Home Front in World War II by Stewart Ross (Hodder Wayland, 2002)

I Can Remember World War Two by S. Hewitt (Watts Books, 2003)

My War: ARP Volunteer by Stewart Ross (Hodder Wayland, 2005)

My War: Evacuee by Peter Hepplewhite (Hodder Wayland, 2005)

My War: Home Guard by Philip Steele (Hodder Wayland, 2005)

Websites

http://www.bbc.co.uk/history/ww2children/
Includes a tour around a wartime home, complete with Anderson shelter, a rationing challenge and extracts from letters written to evacuees.

The website addresses (URLs) included in this book were valid at the time of going to press. However, because of the nature of the Internet, it is possible that some addresses may have changed, or sites may have changed or closed down since publication. While the author and publisher regret any inconvenience this may cause the readers, no responsibility for any such changes can be accepted by either the author or the publisher.

Places to Visit

Chislehurst Caves
Old Hill
Chislehurst
Kent
BR7 5NB
Phone: (020) 8467 3264
Fax (020) 8295 0407
Email: enquiries@chislehurstcaves.co.uk
Guided tours of the caves used as air-raid shelters.

Eden Camp Modern History Theme Museum
Malton
North Yorkshire
YO17 6RT
Telephone: 01653 697777
Fax: 01653 698243
E-mail: admin@edencamp.co.uk

Imperial War Museum London (Headquarters)
Lambeth Road
London SE1 6HZ
Phone: (020) 7416 5320
Fax: (020) 7416 5374
Email: mail@iwm.org.uk

Imperial War Museum North
The Quays
Trafford Wharf
Trafford Park
Manchester M17 1TE
Phone: 0161 836 4000
Fax: 0161 836 4012
Email: iwmnorth@iwm.org.uk

Acknowledgements

Page 5 *The Day War Broke Out* by Peter Haining (W. H. Allen and Co, 1989)

Page 9 *No Time to Say Goodbye* by Ben Wicks (Bloomsbury, 1986)

Page 10 *The World is a Wedding* by Bernard Kops (Valentine, Mitchell and Co, 1973)

Pages 13, 34 *War Boy: A Country Childhood* by Michael Foreman (Pavilion Books, 1989)

Page 15 *We'll Eat Again: A Collection of Recipes from the War Years* by Marguerite Patten (Hamlyn, 1985)

Page 19 *Children of the Blitz* by Robert Westall (Penguin, 1987)

Page 23, 24 *The Greenock Blitz* (Inverclyde District Libraries, 1991)

Page 31 *A Child's War* by Molly Bihet (Private publication)

Pages 33, 41 *Liberation* by Nick Machon (The Guernsey Press, 1985)

Page 36 *A People's War* by Peter Lewis (Methuen, 1986)

Pages 43, 45 *We'll Meet Again* by Vera Lynn with Robin Cross and Jenny De Gex (Sidgwick and Jackson, 1989)

Index